Crinkleroot's

25 MORE ANIMALS

EVERY CHILD SHOULD KNOW

BY JIM ARNOSKY

BRADBURY PRESS   NEW YORK

Maxwell Macmillan Canada   Toronto
Maxwell Macmillan International
New York   Oxford   Singapore   Sydney

To Maureen Hayes

A NOTE FROM THE AUTHOR

In his *Book of Woodcraft* the great naturalist Ernest Thompson Seton listed forty birds that he thought every child should know. Though I disagreed with some of his selections, the listing made me think: How many and which birds should every child know? Which fish? Which mammals? What other animals?

The four books in the series CRINKLEROOT'S 100 ANIMALS EVERY CHILD SHOULD KNOW (*Crinkleroot's 25 Birds, 25 Fish, 25 Mammals,* and *25 More Animals*) are intended to provide a base of knowledge of the animal kingdom. I hope my selections will make parents and teachers consider, as Mr. Seton's forty birds made me consider, which other animals should be included.

—Jim Arnosky

Bradbury Press
Macmillan Publishing Company
866 Third Avenue
New York, NY 10022

Maxwell Macmillan Canada, Inc.
1200 Eglinton Avenue East
Suite 200
Don Mills, Ontario M3C 3N1

Macmillan Publishing Company is part of the
Maxwell Communication Group of Companies.

First edition
Printed and bound in the United States of America
10 9 8 7 6 5 4 3 2 1
The text is set in ITC Bookman Light. Typography by Julie Quan

Printed on recycled paper

LIBRARY OF CONGRESS CATALOGING-IN-PUBLICATION DATA
Arnosky, Jim.
Crinkleroot's 25 more animals every child should know / by Jim Arnosky.—1st ed.
p.   cm.
Summary: The jovial woodsman Crinkleroot introduces twenty-five realistically drawn animals, including the frog, starfish, and grasshopper.
ISBN 0-02-705846-8
1. Animals—Juvenile literature. 2. Animals—Identification—Juvenile literature. [1. Animals.] I. Title. II. Title: Crinkleroot's twenty-five more animals every child should know.
QL49.A77   1994
591—dc20   93-7584

Hello! My name is Crinkleroot. I'm always on the lookout for animals. How many different kinds of animals do you know? In this book there are twenty-five animals you should know.

Some live right around your home—
in the park, or in your own
backyard. Some even live in
your house!

Some live underground.

Some live in the sea.

The earth is home to all kinds of animals.
Some are big. Some are small. Be like
me and learn them all!

Your friend,

Crinkleroot

Frog

Toad

Salamander

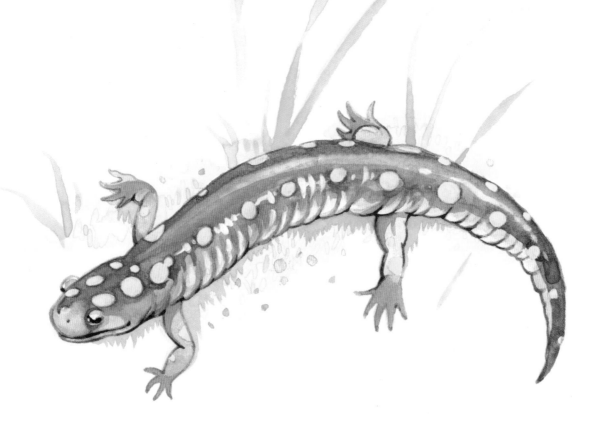

Lizard

Turtle

Alligator

Snake

Worm

Snail

Clam

Crab

Lobster

Octopus

Starfish

Spider

Tick

Caterpillar

Butterfly

Cricket

Grasshopper

Beetle

Ant

Bee

Dragonfly

Housefly

GR